BRAIN BOOSTERS

SPACE PUZZLES

by
Vicky Barker
& Ste Johnson

LiTtle
GENIUS
BOoks

Published by Little Genius Books. www.littlegeniusbooks.com. • 10 9 8 7 6 5 4 3 2 1 • 9781953344441

Text and illustrations copyright © 2021 b small publishing ltd. Art Director: Vicky Barker. Editorial: Sam Hutchinson. Printed in China by WKT Co. Ltd.

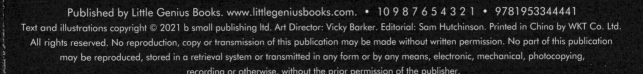

Which rocket reached the moon first?

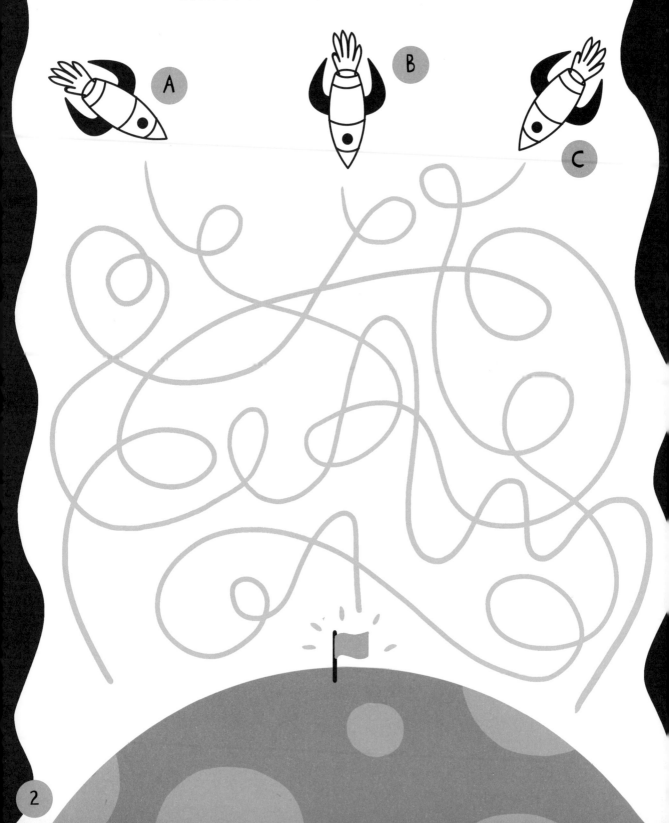

Doodle some details on these aliens!

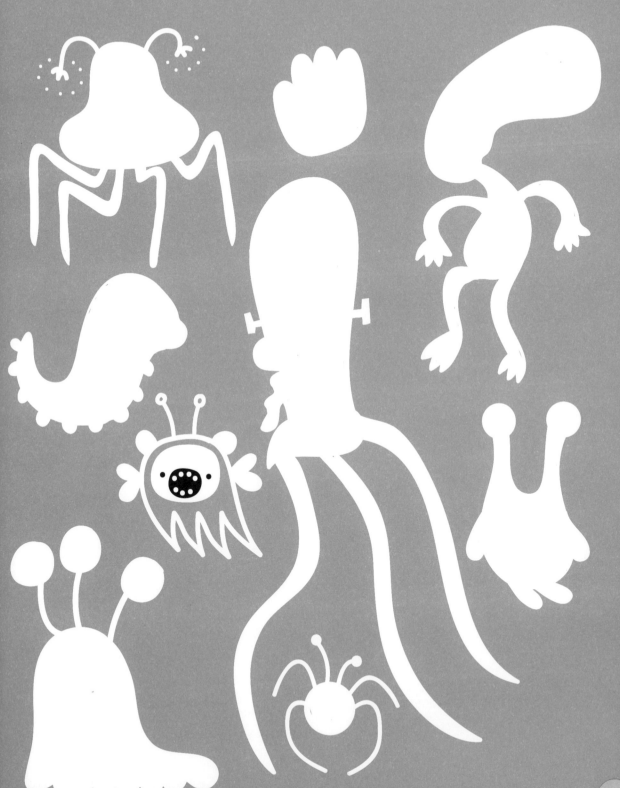

Venus

Mercury

Color in the planets.
Cover the page and try to remember the correct order.

Earth

Jupiter

Neptune

Mars

Saturn

Uranus

What can you see out of the spacecraft window?

This word search is out of this world.

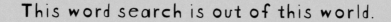

S	P	U	I	V	A	S	T	R	O	N	A	U	T	H	H	K
U	S	C	J	H	U	K	T	C	O	C	K	P	I	T	N
N	S	Q	S	P	F	C	S	E	V	X	H	W	R	A	E
I	P	O	P	W	R	U	M	T	F	M	H	S	K	X	I
V	A	H	A	I	N	J	I	Q	L	E	A	P	T	M	L
E	C	F	C	V	D	B	B	L	M	T	X	L	L	J	A
R	E	S	E	D	R	P	E	T	H	E	H	A	E	H	C
S	S	T	F	O	M	L	E	A	R	O	C	N	M	S	A
E	H	A	B	X	G	K	X	P	O	R	X	E	V	R	L
Y	I	R	G	S	C	F	K	C	O	M	E	T	A	A	H
F	P	S	L	O	W	N	N	K	U	O	U	L	W	R	J
E	U	B	R	L	E	O	G	D	V	P	O	X	U	K	M
A	L	G	X	J	F	O	J	L	M	S	K	E	L	P	P
R	F	A	X	E	A	M	S	H	G	A	L	A	X	Y	X
T	C	L	S	A	S	T	E	R	O	I	D	E	K	P	T
H	Z	S	A	T	E	L	L	I	T	E	M	K	R	A	D

SPACE	COMET	SUN	SATELLITE
PLANET	EARTH	SOLAR	UNIVERSE
STAR	MOON	SPACESHIP	ORBIT
ROCKET	GALAXY	COCKPIT	ASTEROID
ALIEN	ASTRONAUT	METEOR	DARK

Are there more blue stars or orange comets?

8

Design a cool
space suit!

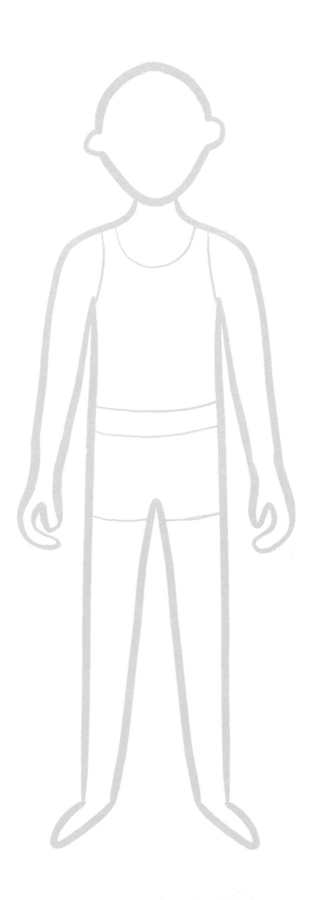

DID YOU KNOW?

The coating on the
outside of an
astronaut's visor
is made of gold.

True or false?

1. There are nine planets in the solar system.

2. On Venus, one day lasts longer than one year.

3. Jupiter has over 70 moons.

4. Mars is a gas giant.

5. Mercury is hotter than Venus.

6. It takes just over eight minutes for light from the Sun to reach us on Earth.

Follow the path of the space shuttle to find out where it is heading.

Space Team, Captain's Log:

My team arrived on the unexplored, alien planet
to the sound of a very strange noise.
We slowly approached to learn more...

_____

_____

_____

_____

_____

_____

_____

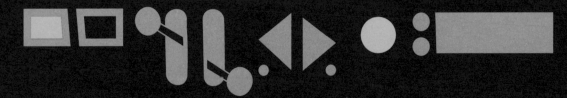

How many visitors have been to this moon? Count the different footprints.

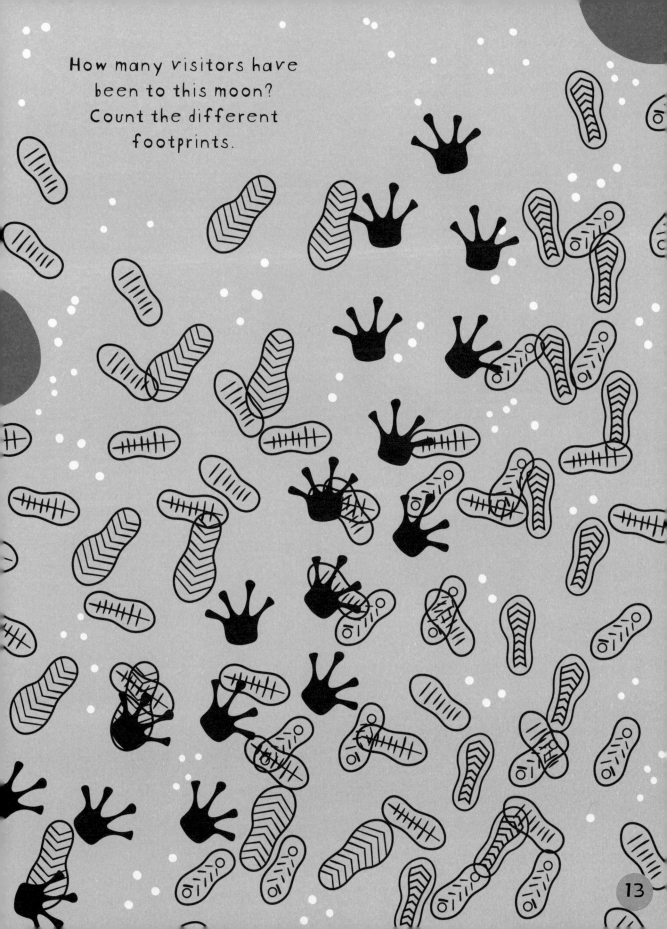

Help this alien spacecraft navigate
through the space dust.

HOME

14

Draw the other half of this space shuttle.

Connect the dots to reveal this space scene.

One of these space suits is unique.
Can you spot which one?

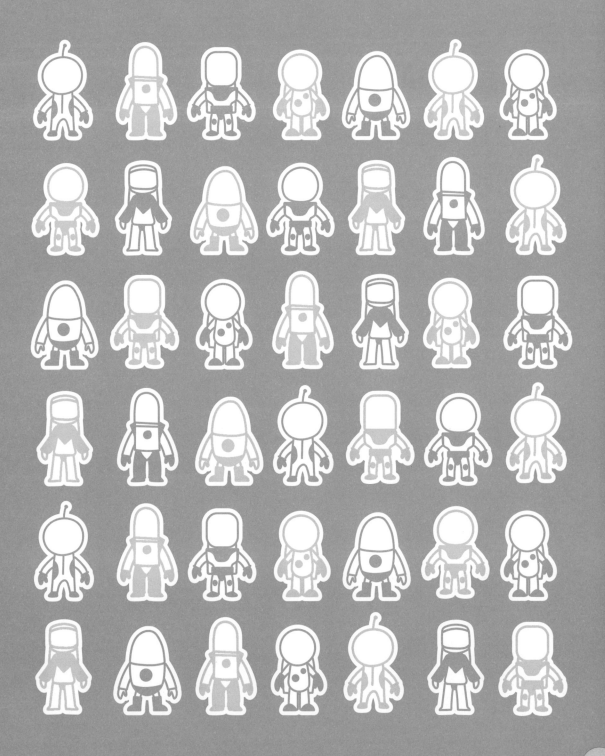

Find the group of planets that matches the group on the right.

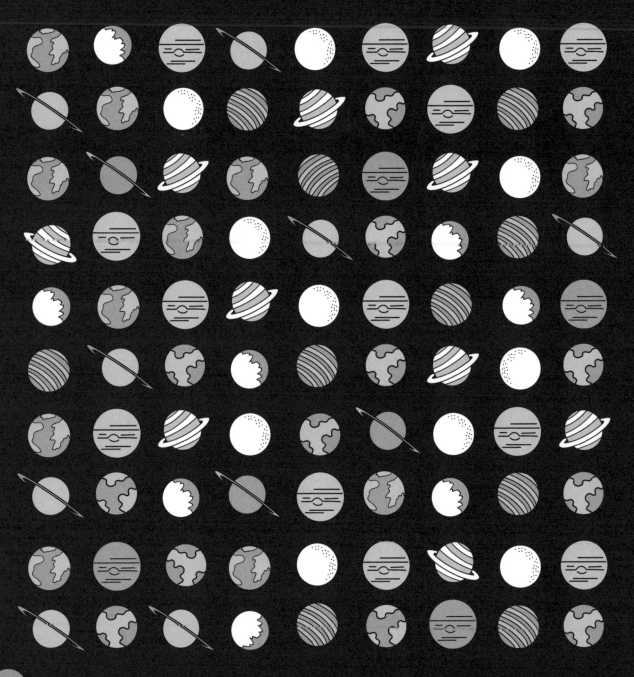

Subtract all of the spaces with a dot marked in them by coloring them in. You will reveal a picture in the spaces left behind!

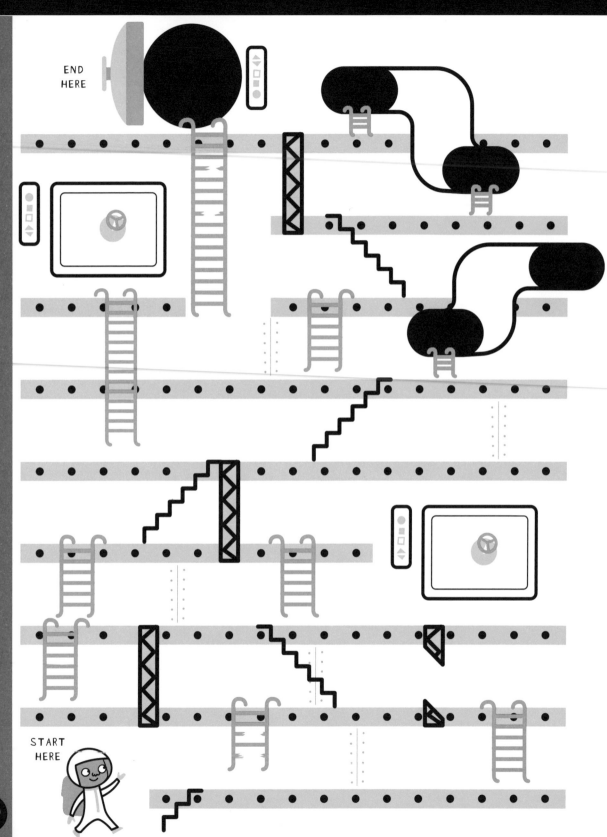

END HERE

START HERE

Use this step-by-step guide to draw
a super-powered rocket ship below.

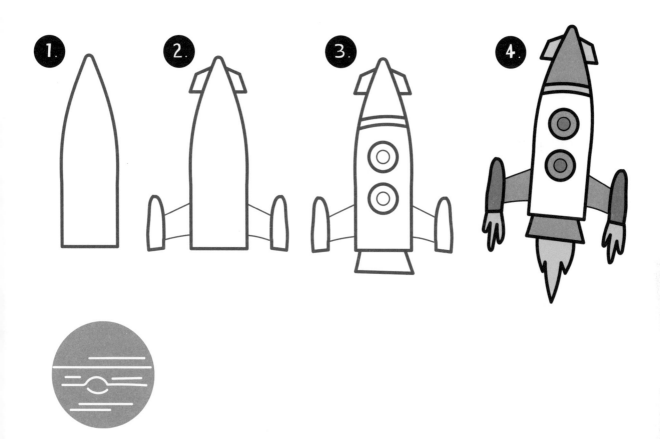

Design your own cool spaceship!

What would you call it?

Match these satellites to their shadows.

Can you work out the answers to these sums?

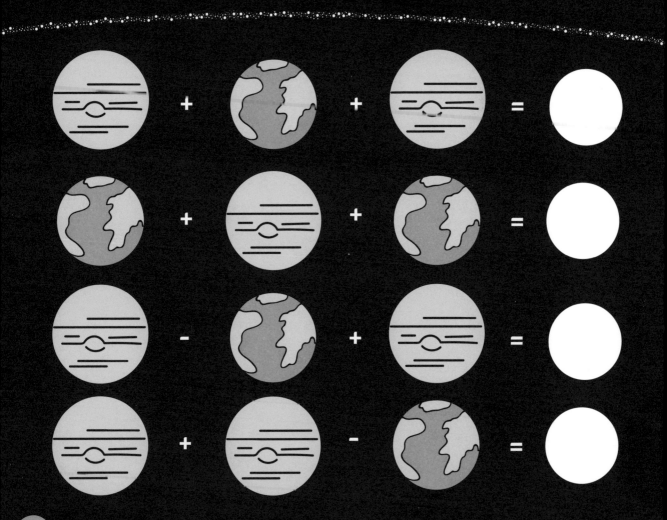

Copy these aliens onto the empty grids and color them in.

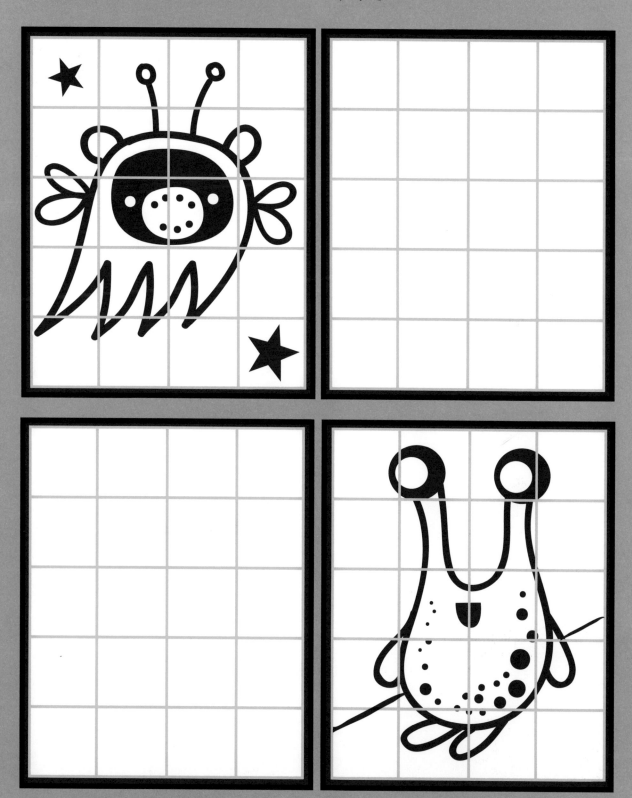

Astronauts aboard the space station are receiving a message. Color in each of the squares in this list to reveal the image.

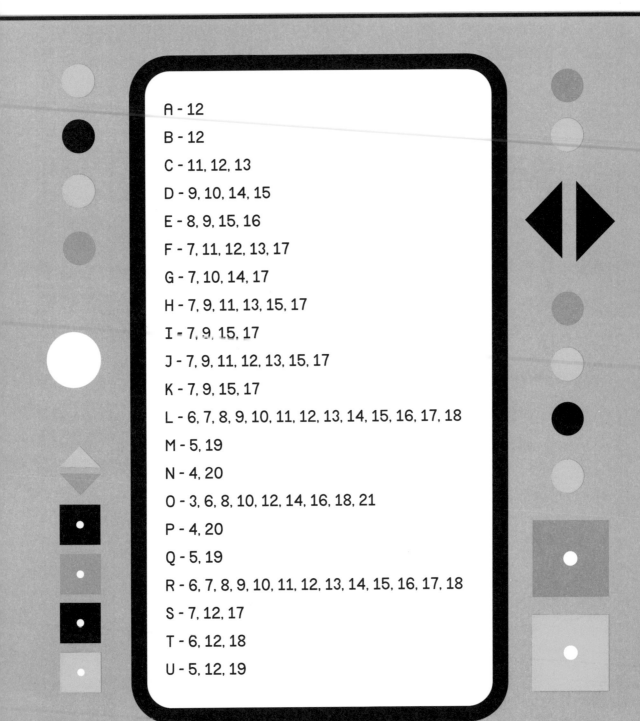

A - 12
B - 12
C - 11, 12, 13
D - 9, 10, 14, 15
E - 8, 9, 15, 16
F - 7, 11, 12, 13, 17
G - 7, 10, 14, 17
H - 7, 9, 11, 13, 15, 17
I - 7, 9, 15, 17
J - 7, 9, 11, 12, 13, 15, 17
K - 7, 9, 15, 17
L - 6, 7, 8, 9, 10, 11, 12, 13, 14, 15, 16, 17, 18
M - 5, 19
N - 4, 20
O - 3, 6, 8, 10, 12, 14, 16, 18, 21
P - 4, 20
Q - 5, 19
R - 6, 7, 8, 9, 10, 11, 12, 13, 14, 15, 16, 17, 18
S - 7, 12, 17
T - 6, 12, 18
U - 5, 12, 19

	1	2	3	4	5	6	7	8	9	10	11	12	13	14	15	16	17	18	19	20	21	22	23	24
A																								
B																								
C																								
D																								
E																								
F																								
G																								
H																								
I																								
J																								
K																								
L																								
M																								
N																								
O																								
P																								
Q																								
R																								
S																								
T																								
U																								

Starting at Sun and without taking your pen off the page, follow the letters around until you find each of the eight planets in our solar system.

START HERE →

SUNMERCURY
UJSRAMHTRV
PITERSATAE
NEPTUNEUEN
SUNARUNRSU

DID YOU KNOW?

Pluto used to be the ninth planet but is now classed as a DWARF PLANET.

What is the correct sequence for takeoff?

1 ☐ 2 ☐ 3 ☐ 4 ☐ 5 ☐

Each of these sets of stars has a different number pattern. Can you work out the pattern and fill in the blank spaces?

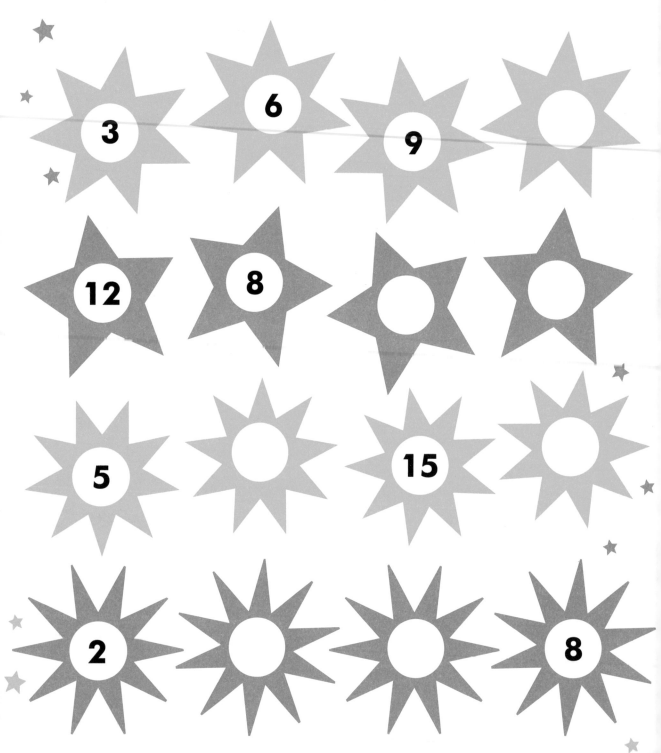

This space shuttle is delivering important cargo. How quickly can you get it there? Draw a line as fast as you can without going off the path. Time yourself!

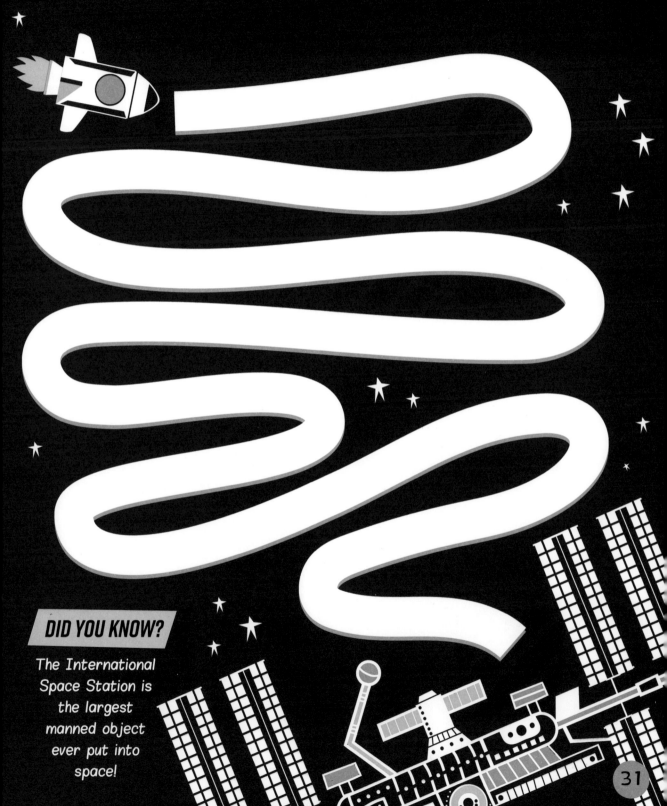

DID YOU KNOW?

The International Space Station is the largest manned object ever put into space!

Can you work out the code to launch the space shuttle?
Fill in the missing shapes in the sequence to
commence liftoff.

How many complete space suits can you put together with these items below?

DID YOU KNOW?

Space suits are puncture proof.

What is out of place in this scene?

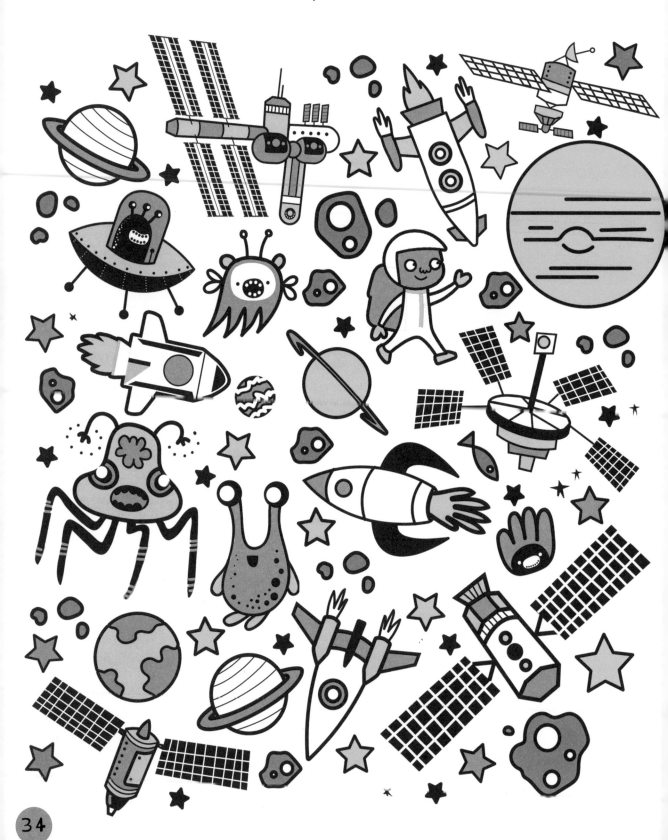

Is there an odd or even number of stars below?
Count them and find out!

DID YOU KNOW?

*Small stars live longer
than large stars.*

Spot ten differences in these cockpit scenes.

Can you find these squares in the picture below?

QUICK QUIZ!

1. Who was the first person on the moon?
   a) Mary Footstrong   b) Neil Armstrong
   c) Dave Handstrong   d) Agnes Headstrong

2. How many miles is it to the Sun from Earth on average throughout the year?
   a) 93 miles   b) 9,300 miles
   c) 930,000 miles   d) 93,000,000 miles

3. How many planets in our solar system have rings?
   a) 0   b) 4   c) 2   d) 3

4. What is the name of our solar system?
   a) Milky Bay   b) Milky Way
   c) Milky Say   d) Milky Tea

5. How hot is the center of the Sun?
   a) 2,700 degrees F   b) 27,000 degrees F
   c) 270,000 degrees F   d) 27,000,000 degrees F

Which space shuttle gets back to Earth first?
Work out the sums. The one with the highest total wins!
Use a separate piece of paper if you need to.

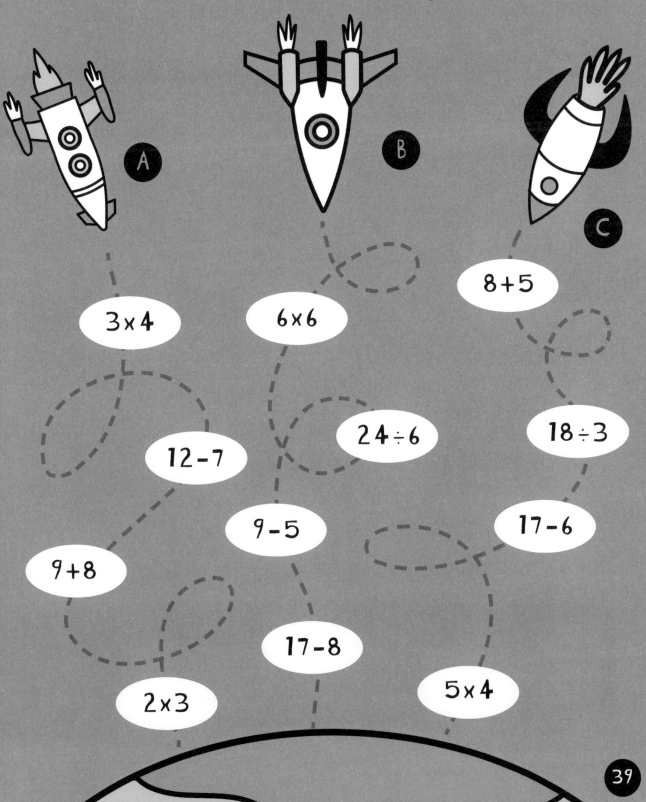

A

B

C

8 + 5

3 x 4

6 x 6

24 ÷ 6

18 ÷ 3

12 − 7

9 − 5

17 − 6

9 + 8

17 − 8

5 x 4

2 x 3

Can you find the row that matches the silhouette?

You have discovered a new planet in your space exploration!
Draw or write what it looks like and who might live there.
Can you give it a name?

DID YOU KNOW?

An exoplanet is a planet found
outside of our solar system.
There have been over 4,000
discovered so far.

Spot ten differences in this scene.

Help navigate this spaceship along the gray path safely away from the black hole!

SAFETY

Can you complete this picture grid? Fill in each of the boxes with one of the four pictures. Every column, row, and four-square block must contain one of each.

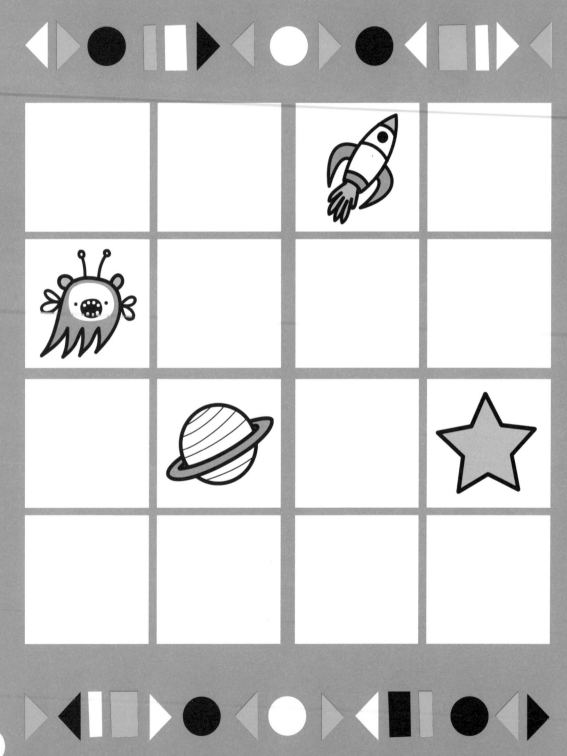

Can you add craters to the moons so that
each row (across, down, and diagonal) adds up to 15?

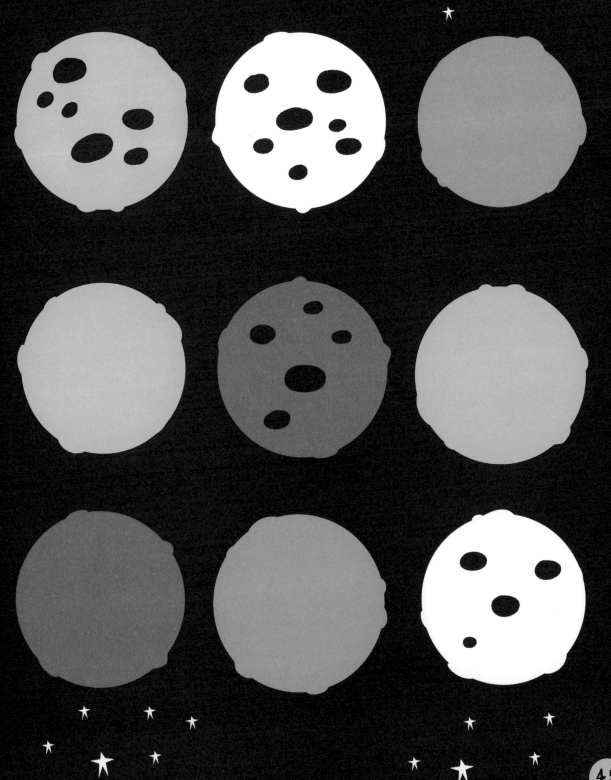

Answers

Page 2

Page 14

Page 7

S	P	U	I	V	A	S	T	R	O	N	A	U	T	H	K
U	S	C	J	H	U	K	T	C	O	C	K	P	I	T	N
N	S	Q	S	P	F	C	S	E	V	X	H	W	R	A	E
I	P	O	P	W	R	U	M	T	F	M	H	S	K	X	L
V	A	H	A	I	N	J	I	Q	L	E	A	P	T	M	L
E	C	F	C	V	D	B	L	M	T	X	L	L	J	A	A
R	E	S	E	D	R	P	E	T	H	E	H	A	E	H	C
S	S	T	F	O	M	L	E	A	R	O	C	N	M	S	H
E	H	I	B	X	G	K	Y	P	O	R	X	E	V	R	L
Y	F	P	S	C	F	K	C	O	M	E	T	A	A	H	C
F	P	S	L	O	W	N	N	K	U	O	U	L	W	R	J
E	U	B	R	L	E	O	G	D	V	P	O	X	U	K	M
A	L	G	X	J	F	O	J	L	M	S	K	E	L	P	P
R	R	F	A	X	E	A	M	S	H	G	A	L	A	X	Y	X
T	C	L	S	A	S	T	E	R	O	I	D	E	K	P	T
H	Z	S	A	T	E	L	L	I	T	E	M	K	R	A	D

Page 16

Page 17

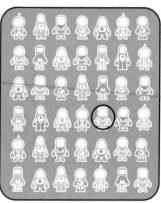

Page 18

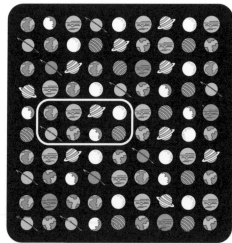

Page 8 – There are more blue stars.

Page 10 – 1. False   2. True   3. True
         4. False   5. False   6. True

Page 11 – **THE RINGED PLANET**

Page 13

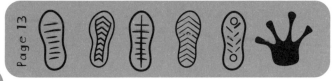

Page 19

Page 20

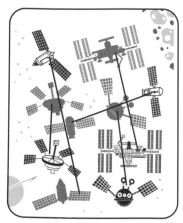

Pages 26-27

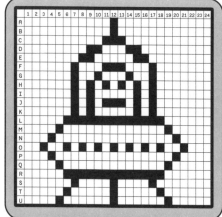

Page 28

S U N M E R C U R Y
U J S R A M H T R V
P I T E R S A T A E
N E P T U N E U E N
S U N A R U N R S U

Page 29
1. C 2. D 3. E 4. B 5. A

Page 30

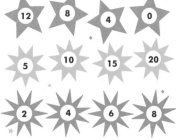

Page 32

Page 33

You can make nine complete space suits.

Page 34

Page 23

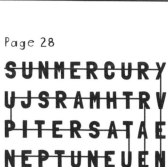

Page 24

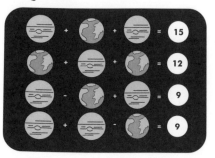

Page 35

ODD. There are 15 stars.
6 ORANGE
9 BLUE

Page 36

Page 37

Page 42

Page 43

Page 38

1. B
2. D
3. B
4. B
5. D

Page 39

A = 40   B = 53   C = 50

B reaches Earth first.

Page 44

Page 45

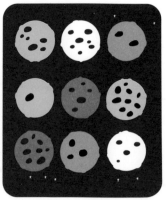

Page 40 - Row 4